SHARK ENCOUNTERS

by Bob Woods

Stride

An Imprint of The Child's World®

childsworld.com

The Child's World
childsworld.com

Published by The Child's World®
800-599-READ • www.childsworld.com

Photography Credits
Cover: Martin Prochazkacz/Shutterstock.
Interior: AP/Images: Dennis Fujimoto 18; Lucy Pemoni 19.
Dreamstime: Antpun 12; Wirestock 15; Eyewave 23; Wonderful
Nature 24T. Mike Eliason: 16. National Marine Fisheries Agency:
9B. NOAA: 28. Shutterstock: Sergey Uryadnikov 5; Racksuz 6;
Natursports 7; Martin Prochazkacz 8; Tomas Kotouc 9T; Frhojdysz
10; Bearacreative 11T; Martin Prochazkacz 11B, 13T, 27B;
Wildestanimal 13B, 29; Eskymaks 14; Richard Condlyffe 16; Bert
Folsom 19T; Stefan Pircher 19B; Natalia Paklina 24B; Nicholas
Floyd 25; HainaultPhoto 26; VisionDive 27T.

ISBN Information
9781503858176 (Reinforced Library Binding)
9781503860766 (Portable Document Format)
9781503862128 (Online Multi-user eBook)
9781503863484 (Electronic Publication)

LCCN 2021952455

Printed in the United States of America

TABLE OF CONTENTS

CHAPTER 1

SHOULD YOU BE AFRAID?

A quiet day at the beach . . . when suddenly—SHARK! Lifeguards' whistles shriek. Panicked swimmers run out of the water. Then everyone stands on the beach, scanning the ocean surface for the telltale fin of the shark!

Nature shows and movies about these man-eating monsters are wildly popular. When there is a shark **encounter**, the **media** report on it for days. Some people decide never to swim at the beach.

As with so many things we fear, though, the truth about sharks is not nearly so scary. Sharks are really not that dangerous—at least if you're a human.

Some sharks, like this great white, can leap out of the ocean.

Based on fossils, this is what an ancient shark called Megalodon might have looked like.

Sharks began roaming Earth's oceans over 400 million years ago—long before the age of the dinosaurs. Today, *T. rex* is long gone, but sharks such as the great white, tiger shark, and bull shark live on. Among the 500 types of sharks, those three are involved in most of the encounters with humans.

Shark encounters are extremely rare. At the beach, you're at much greater risk of getting hurt from sunburn! You might also get stung by a **jellyfish**, cut your foot on a seashell, or get in trouble while you're swimming.

Often the only part of a shark that can be seen when it is swimming is the top fin.

A person's chances of being killed by a shark are very, very small. In the United States, bee and wasp stings cause about 50 deaths each year. Nearly 700 people die from bicycle accidents.

In 2020, only three people died because of a shark bite in the U.S. While that is very tragic, the low number shows just how rare shark encounters are.

Great whites have a huge mouth filled with razor-sharp teeth.

The great white shark, star of the movie *Jaws*, is the most famous type of shark. Its open mouth reveals huge, sharp teeth. A fin shaped like a triangle sits atop its grey, torpedo-shaped body.

A great white can grow to around 20 feet (6 m) long, weigh 5,000 pounds (2,268 kg), and have 3,000 teeth!

All sharks are fish. The smallest **species** is the dwarf lanternshark, at about six inches (15 cm). The largest is the whale shark, which averages 45 feet (14 m) long and weighs 24,000 pounds (10,886 kg). Also, unlike most fish, sharks don't have bones. Their skeletons are made of **cartilage**— the same tough, flexible tissue that forms your nose and ears.

Most sharks have a narrow body shape with a large tail and a pointed nose. Some sharks have special features. The sawshark has a long, flat snout edged with sharp teeth. And check out the hammerhead's unusual wide head, with an eye on each side!

Eyes on each side of its head help the hammerhead find prey.

Shark tails vary, too. A boomerang shape helps the fastest shark, the mako, reach speeds of up to 60 miles per hour (97 kmh). The thresher shark's sword-shaped tail can grow to eight feet (2 m) long. Many sharks have gray skin. Some have spots or stripes.

(Top) A thresher shark's tail can be as long as its body. (Bottom) The speedy mako shark can track down any meal.

11

The vivid green eyes of this shark see well underwater.

Sharks have black, green, or gold eyes. They see in color, and have very good eyesight. Their "ears" are actually two tiny openings on top of their heads. Sharks have keen senses of smell and taste, too.

Sharks are **predators**. That means they eat other animals. Different kinds of sharks have different kinds of teeth, depending on what **prey** they eat.

For instance, tiger and great white sharks use their super-sharp teeth to rip into fish, seals, and sea turtles—and, on very rare occasions, people.

Dangerous bull sharks live not only in warm ocean waters, but also in freshwater rivers. They have been spotted in the Mississippi River, as far north as Illinois!

Often seen near beaches, tiger sharks are one of the fiercest species of sharks.

CHAPTER 2

HOW ENCOUNTERS HAPPEN

Sharks can be **aggressive** hunters, but they do not hunt for humans. Of the hundreds of shark species, only about 30 are known to have bitten people. Every day, millions of people swim, dive, or fish in waters where sharks live. Even so, only about 50 are bitten each year.

Some species of sharks swim in shallow water near beaches.

Scientists at the University of Florida have conducted a worldwide study of shark encounters. In 2020, they counted 57 **unprovoked** encounters—those in which the shark, not the person, made first contact. Ten of those victims died.

A blacktip reef shark moves into a school of smaller fish, who are clearly heading for safety!

There are two different kinds of unprovoked shark encounters with humans. Most happen near beaches. The sharks find fish in these waters, but there are also swimmers, divers, and surfers. Big waves and strong **currents** churn up the shallow water. In those **murky** waters, a shark can mistake a moving human for a fish. Usually, the shark takes a quick bite and moves on. The person's injuries are often minor.

A few bump-and-bite encounters happen in deeper water, where the person doesn't see the shark before it strikes. It might bump the person first, then bite, again and again. Bites like these can cause serious injury or death.

A pair of sharks swim very near the beach in Carpinteria, California.

Great whites look for large fish and marine mammals to eat.

Although great whites are the most feared sharks, most people who encounter them live to tell their tales. It seems that these sharks don't particularly care for the taste of humans. Nonetheless, great whites are feared as killers that could rip swimmers to shreds.

That's a **myth**. A shark's many teeth and powerful jaws can turn a big, fat seal into fast food, but humans aren't on the great white's menu. If a great white does take a bite out of a person, it usually spits out the piece and moves on. We're too bony!

Hard, pointed shark teeth

WHAT'S IN THE CAGE?

Scuba divers can get very close to sharks by protecting themselves with strong metal cages. These cages are used by scientists and photographers.

Tales of surviving shark encounters are both fascinating and frightening. On October 31, 2003, a 14-foot (4-m) tiger shark bit 13-year-old champion surfer Bethany Hamilton in Hawai'i. She lost her left arm, but not her spirit.

This is Bethany Hamilton's surfboard after her encounter with a shark.

"My arm was hanging in the water, and the shark just came and bit me," she told a reporter. "But I just held onto my board and then it let go." The shark swam away. Luckily, Bethany was surfing with her dad. He quickly got her back to shore and saved her life.

Just 10 weeks later, Bethany was back on a surfboard and getting ready to compete again—and she won!

Even with one arm, Bethany returned to surfing events.

CHAPTER 3

YOU AND SHARKS

The odds of coming face-to-face with a shark are tiny—even if you often go to the beach. But what if you do see one? Would you know how to avoid danger?

Here are some tips from shark experts for whenever you go in the ocean:

- At the beach, don't wander too far from shore.
- Avoid swimming alone. Be sure parents and lifeguards can see you.
- If the waves are big and the water is murky, don't splash around too much. A shark feeding in the area might mistake you for a fish.
- Avoid going in the water at dawn, at dusk, or after dark, when sharks like to feed.

Always swim in an area with other people.

23

- Remove shiny jewelry.
- Don't go in the water if you're bleeding.
- Don't swim, dive, or surf near fishing boats. They often throw bait in the water to attract fish—and sometimes sharks.

A shark might mistake this surfer for a seal.

- Beware of sitting on a surfboard in deep water. Dangling arms and legs make you look like a seal from underneath.
- Stay out of areas where sharks have been reported in the past few days or where they regularly feed.

If you do see a shark, never try to touch it. Leave the water immediately. If a shark bites or bumps you, stay calm. Fight back by punching the shark in the eyes or **gills**.

While birds follow this fishing boat in the air, sharks might be in the water below.

Watch for signs that warn of recent shark sightings.

As much as we fear sharks, sharks really should fear us more. After all, sharks only kill a few people each year, while people kill millions of sharks. Many shark species are in danger of becoming **extinct**—dying out altogether.

The greatest human threat to sharks is fishing. Some fisherman catch sharks for sport. Others are after the sharks' cartilage, which is used in some medicines.

This fish market displays sharks being sold for food.

Sharks can be caught up in nets targeted at other kinds of fish.

In some countries, the fins are cut off live sharks—which are then thrown back into the sea to die—and used to make a special soup.

ENDANGERED SHARKS

Scientists have identified more than 140 species of sharks at risk of becoming extinct because they're hunted for food and body parts. Among them are the basking (above), whale, blacktip, and great white sharks.

Marine biologists and environmental groups are working to protect sharks from human abuse. They also are asking governments around the world to ban unnecessary shark fishing.

Larger sharks—such as great white, basking, and whale sharks—face the greatest danger, because they are the ones humans hunt the most. Great white sharks are now protected along the coasts of California and South Africa. They cannot be hunted in those areas.

A scientist measures a shark in the water before releasing it. The more scientists can learn, the better we can protect sharks.

Off the coast of Australia, a great white shark swims while jack fish tag along.

We're learning that sharks aren't really the bloodthirsty killers of popular movies. They're really an important and valuable part of their ocean environment.

By learning more about sharks, we can come to respect these ancient animals and their place in the world.

GLOSSARY

aggressive (uh-GRESS-iv) someone or something that is mean and is often ready to attack

cartilage (KART-ih-lij) flexible, bony material that makes up a shark's body (and your nose and ears)

currents (KUR-ents) constantly flowing water or air

encounter (en-KOWNT-er) a meeting of two things

extinct (eks-TINKT) no longer existing; usually used to describe animals or plants

gills (GILZ) the slits on both sides of a fish's head that it uses to breathe

jellyfish (JEL-ee-fish) a sea creature that has no backbone and an almost clear body; some have long, stinging tentacles

marine biologists (muh-REEN by-ALL-uh-jists) scientists who study animals and plants that live in the sea

media (MEE-dee-ah) all the television and radio networks, newspapers, magazines, and web sites that report news, and the people who work for them

murky (MERK-ee) cloudy or hard to see in

myth (MITH) a story, often an ancient one; a fictional tale

predators (PRED-uh-terz) animals that hunt other animals

prey (PRAY) animals that are eaten by other animals

species (SPEE-sheez) group of closely related plants or animals unprovoked not caused by the person being attacked

unprovoked (un-pruh-VOHKD) one without a specific cause

THINK ABOUT IT

What was the coolest shark you read about in this book? Explain your reasons.

If you were afraid of sharks, did this book make you less afraid? Why or why not?

If sharks weren't in scary movies, do you think people would still be afraid of them? Why or why not?

FIND OUT MORE

IN THE LIBRARY

Crisp, Lauren. *Sharks!* New York, NY: Tiger Tales, 2022.

Doubilet, David. *Face to Face with Sharks*. Washington, DC: National Geographic Kids, 2019.

Harris, Tim. *Predator vs Prey: How Sharks and Other Fish Attack*. London, UK: Wayland Publishing, 2022.

ON THE WEB

Visit our website for links about sharks:
childsworld.com/links

Note to Parents, Teachers, and Librarians:
We routinely verify our Web links to make sure they are safe
and active sites. So encourage your readers to check them out!

INDEX

ABOUT THE AUTHOR

BOB WOODS, who is not afraid to go swimming in the ocean, has written many books for young readers and for adults. He has written about sports, cars and motorcycles, business, and other topics. He lives in Connecticut.